DATE DUE

JAN 2 1			
Clark			
NOV 1 9 '70			
MAY 7 71			
K-3			
DEC 14 74			
K-2			
T-1			
T-3			
APR 19 1978			
JAN 1 8 '83			
JAN 2 4 1990			
MAY 1 6 1990			
MAY 3 0 1990			
Knopp			
APR 2 5 '94			
DEC 1 4 1995			
GAYLORD			PRINTED IN U.S.A

What Is A Turtle

By Gene Darby

Pictures — Lucy and John Hawkinson

BENEFIC PRESS · CHICAGO

Publishing Division of Beckley-Cardy Company

Atlanta   **Dallas**   **Long Beach**   **Portland**

The WHAT IS IT Series

What Is A Plant

What Is A Season

What Is A Turtle

What Is A Bird

What Is A Chicken

What Is A Rock

What Is A Magnet

What Is A Rocket

What Is A Solar System

What Is A Machine

What Is Light

What Is Heat

What Is A Fish

What Is A Butterfly

What Is A Cow

What Is A Frog

What Is A Tree

What Is Air

What Is Gravity

What Is Weather

What Is Electricity

What Is Water

What Is Sound

What Is An Atom

CONTENTS

THIS IS A TURTLE

Painted turtle

A turtle has one head.
It can turn its head.

It can turn its head like this.

It can turn its head like this.

6

A turtle can put its head up.

It can put its head down.

7

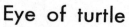
Eye of turtle

A turtle has two eyes.

It can open its eyes.

It can close its eyes.

8

A turtle sees food with its eyes.

A turtle sees where it is going.

A turtle can see in the water.
It can see through its eye lid.

A turtle has one nose.
It smells with its nose.
It smells food.

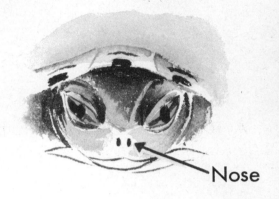

Nose

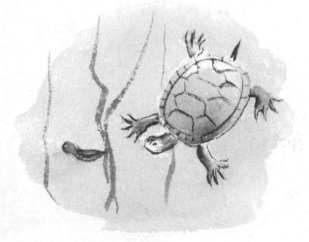

It smells with its nose
under water.

It smells with its nose
out of water.

A turtle has two ears.
You can not see its ears.
Its ears are inside.

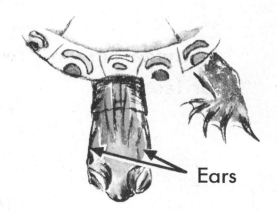

Ears

A turtle has one mouth.
A turtle has no teeth,
but its jaws have sharp edges.

A turtle has one, two, three,
four feet.

A turtle has one tail.

A turtle lives in a shell.
The top of the shell looks
like this.

But, look under the shell.
It looks like this.

The edges of the shell
come together.

WHAT CAN A TURTLE DO?

Look at the turtle.
What can it do?

See what the turtle can do.
Where are its feet?
Where is its head?
Where is its tail?

See the turtle walk
on its four feet.

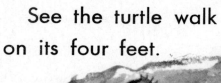

It can walk up.

It can walk down.

See the turtle eat.

The turtle eats this,

and this,

and this.

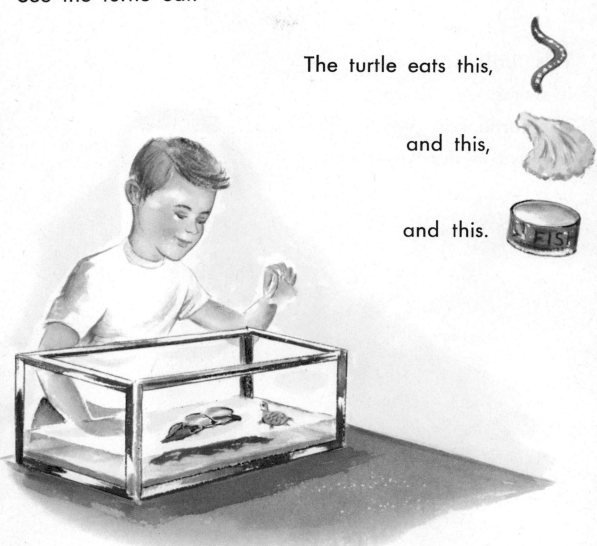

This turtle can swim.
It swims with its feet.
The turtle can play.
It plays in the water.

The turtle swims up
in the water.

It swims down
in the water.

BABY TURTLES

Mother turtles lay eggs.
This mother turtle digs a hole
in the soft ground.
She will lay her eggs
in this hole.

Some mother turtles dig a hole
in the sand for their eggs.

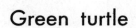

Green turtle

This mother turtle did not
dig a hole.

Common musk turtle

This mother turtle has five
eggs in her nest.
Some turtles lay twenty eggs.
Some sea turtles lay many,
many eggs.

The mother turtle covers the eggs.

She walks on the ground.
Walk, walk, walk.
She makes the ground hard.

The mother turtle goes away.
She goes away to the water.
She will not come back
to her nest.

The sun shines on the ground.
The ground is warm.
The ground warms the eggs.
The eggs stay in the ground
for two or three months.
The eggs are in the ground longer
when it is cold.

Baby turtles come out
of the warm eggs.
See the funny baby turtles.
The baby turtles have a soft shell.
The shell will soon be hard.

A baby turtle looks
much like its mother.

The baby turtles go away
from the nest.
They go to find food.

TURTLES IN WINTER

It is winter.
The ground is cold.
The water is cold.
What will the turtle do?
The turtle is cold, too.

29

The turtle digs a hole.
The turtle digs in the ground
near the water.

The turtle goes down
in the hole.

It is not so cold down
in the ground.

The turtle will sleep
all winter in the hole.

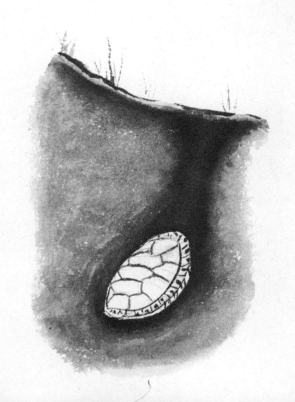

This turtle sleeps all winter, too.
It sleeps in the soft ground
under the water.

Common snapping turtle

This turtle digs a hole, too,
when the winter comes.

It digs in the ground . . . .
just a little.

Common box turtle

The ground is MORE cold.
The turtle digs MORE.

It is colder now.
The ground gets colder.
The turtle gets colder.
Down goes the turtle . . . . down,

down,

down.

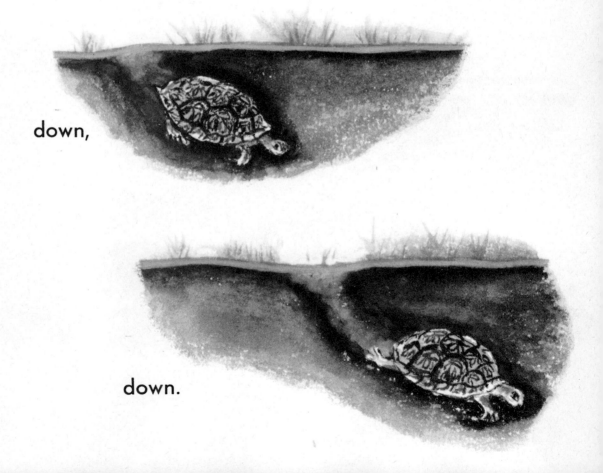

The turtle goes down
where it is not so cold.
   It is not so cold down
in the ground.

The turtle goes to sleep.
Good night, turtle.
Sleep all winter.
Get up when it is warm again.

34

LAND TURTLES

This turtle lives only on land.
It lives on the sand.

Desert tortoise

The sun shines.
It is hot on top of the sand.
It is too hot for a turtle.
Where can the turtle go?

The turtle can go under the hot sand.
Dig, dig, dig.
It digs a hole in the sand.

Winter comes.

The ground is not hot.

It is cold.

Dig, dig, dig.

This turtle digs in winter, too.

It makes a very big hole.

More turtles come.

They come to keep warm.

They sleep here all winter.

The turtle may go
for a walk.
It goes for a walk
to find food.
Rain may fall on the sand.
Some rain falls in a hole.
The turtle can drink.

This turtle makes a nest near her hole.

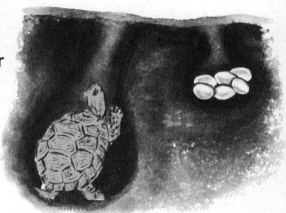

The baby turtles look like their mothers.

The baby turtles can dig like their mothers, too.
See the mother's feet.
See the baby's feet.

These turtles live on land, too.
Sometimes they go to the water
to drink.

Box turtle

Wood turtle

SEA TURTLES

The green turtle lives only
in the water.
It is very, very big.

41

The green turtle eats plants.
It eats plants that are
in the water.

The green turtle goes to land
only to lie in the sun or to lay
its eggs.

This turtle lays many eggs.
Look! See the eggs!

The green turtle's eggs are
this big.

Baby green turtle

These baby turtles look like their mothers.

They will live in the water and eat water plants, too.

Mother green turtle

See the baby turtle's feet.
See the mother turtle's feet.
They swim with these feet.

This is a sea turtle, too.

Hawksbill turtle

This turtle gives us
many pretty things.

45

Turtles give us food.

Some turtles make good pets.

Turtles eat harmful insects.

A turtle is MORE than a shell and four legs.

A turtle is MORE than a head and a tail.

A turtle is a HELPER.

Vocabulary

The total vocabulary of this book is 150 words, excluding proper names. Of these, 49 words (listed below in roman type) are first-grade level; 15 words (listed below in italic type) are above first-grade level. The remaining words are below first-grade level. The words are listed in alphabetical order, and the numbers indicate the pages on which the words first appear.

close 8
cold 24
covers 22

digs 19
drink 38

ears 11
edges 11
eyes 8

fall 38
feet 12
five 21
food 9

goes 23
ground 19

hard 22
harmful 46

helper 46
hole 19
hot 36

insects 46
inside 11
its 6

jaws 11
just 32

keep 37

land 35
lay 19
legs 46
lid 9
lie 42
longer 24

many 21
months 24
more 32
mouth 11
much 26

near 30
nest 21
nose 10

only 35
or 24

plants 42

rain 38

sand 20
sea 21
sharp 11
shell 13

shines 24
smells 10
soft 19
sometimes 40
stay 24
swim 18

teeth 11
than 46
their 20
these 40
through 9
together 13
top 13
turn 6
turtle 5

warm 24
winter 29

SCIENTIFIC NAMES OF TURTLES

The following turtles, listed by both their popular and scientific names, are illustrated in this book. The numbers indicate the pages on which the illustrations appear.

Box turtle 32-34, 40 Terrapene carolina
Common musk turtle 20 Sternotherus odoratus
Common snapping turtle 31 Chelydra serpentina
Desert tortoise 35-39 Gopherus agassizi

Green turtle 20, 41-44 Chelonia mydas
Hawksbill turtle 45 Eretmochelys imbricata
Painted turtle 4-19, 21-23, 25-28, 30, 46-47 Chrysemys picta
Wood turtle 40 Clemmys insculpta